PORTUGAL: PORTUGUESE TRAVEL PHRASEBOOK

The Complete Portuguese Phrasebook for Traveling to Portugal.

+ 1000 Phrases for Accommodations, Shopping, Eating, Traveling, and much more!

By Erica Stewart

Note from the Author

Traveling is one of the most enriching experiences, on so many levels. Being able to interact with the locals makes that experience even more enriching, allowing you to connect with new and interesting people, or even live or study overseas. Traveling is in essence a journey to become more open minded about the world, discovering amazing new people in the process.

As an educator for more than 20 years, I'm a fan of teaching languages to others. This book does not pretend to teach you a commanding knowledge of Portuguese, but is an assembly of the most fundamental phrases you will need when traveling to Portugal. Over the course of this book, I will convey enough knowledge of Portuguese so that you will be able to read, listen, and interact with people in Portugal in a way that will inspire confidence. From here, practice will take you to a new level of accomplishments and a lifetime of enjoyment!

Imagine reading Paulo Coelho, Jorge Amado, or Anibal Machado in its original form! Imagine heading out to Porto, Lisboa or a beautiful costal town, fully equipped to interact with the locals! I invite you to read on and begin a fascinating learning experience.

Best,

Erica Stewart

Table of Contents

Introduction

Portuguese is one of the major languages of the world (the sixth most spoken language worldwide), spoken by about 200 million people on four continents. It belongs to a group of languages called "Romance" or "Neo-Latin" that evolved from Latin, the language of Latium in Ancient Italy, or more specifically, the city of Rome.

Countries and territories where Portuguese is official

- Brazil
- Mozambique
- Angola
- Portugal
- Guinea-Bissau
- Equatorial Guinea
- East Timor
- Macau
- Cape Verde
- São Tomé and Príncipe

Countries and territories where Portuguese has a significant/cultural presence

- Goa (India)
- Daman and Diu (India)

Travel Ideas When Visiting Portugal

- **Lisbon** – Lively, hilly port and capital, with historic trolleys, grand squares, fado clubs, fine art, and a salty sailors' quarter topped by a castle.
- **The Algarve** – Portugal's sunny southern coast, strung with the simple fishing village of Salema, the historic "end of the road" of Cape Sagres, the beach-party town of Lagos, and the laid-back resort of Tavira.
- **Sintra** – A striking town, within easy day-tripping distance from Lisbon, known for its fairy-tale castles, verdant hills, and beautiful gardens.
- **Évora** – Whitewashed little college town with big Roman, Moorish, and Portuguese history encircled by its medieval wall.
- **Nazaré and Nearby** - Traditional fishing village turned small-town resort, and jumping-off point for day trips to the monastery at Batalha, the pilgrimage site of Fátima, Portugal's largest church in Alcobaça, and the photogenic walled town of Óbidos.
- **Coimbra** – Portugal's Oxford, home to an Arab-influenced old town and bustling with students from its prestigious university.
- **Porto** – Gritty, urban second city with picturesque riverfront, charming old town, and museums sporting modern architecture.

- **Douro Valley** – Terraced farming valley and birthplace of port wine, with home bases in modern Peso da Régua and workaday Pinhão.

Culture

The 10-million population of Portugal speaks Portuguese, a Romance language which derived from Vulgar Latin. Galician and Mirandese, which are technically classed as separate languages, are spoken by a few thousand people in the north of the country, along the Spanish border.

Portugal's cultural offering has become more diverse in recent years, particularly with the opening of new event venues in the large cities. Portugal has its own art tradition and many small museums and galleries, even in smaller cities. Most cities have cinemas that mostly show English language films. Films and TV programmes are not dubbed, but generally have subtitles in Portuguese.

"Fado", particularly in Lisbon and Coimbra, is known the world over as the national music. Folklore is also fairly rich and varied, ranging from music and costume, inspired by the Celtic north of the country, to the Algarve's *Corridinho*.

There are some themed film festivals and interesting music festivals during the summer, as well as a wide variety of fairs and festivals. These popular events take place throughout the year and in practically all the smaller towns and villages. The commemorations of the popular saints' days which take place in June with processions and festivities in the streets of Lisbon, Oporto and other cities, are particularly interesting and worth a visit.

Differences with English

Portuguese is a Romance language and part of the Indo-European language family. It is closely related to Spanish. The Portuguese spoken in Europe and the Portuguese spoken in Brazil are further apart in terms of pronunciation, spelling and vocabulary than the English spoken in England and the English spoken in the USA.

We can divide the difference between these languages in some categories, and they are: alphabet, phonology, grammar and vocabulary.

Alphabet

The Portuguese alphabet consists of 23 letters (lacking the K, W and Y of the English alphabet), plus 11 letters with diacritics such as the Ç. Punctuation corresponds largely to that in English. The English writing system, therefore, presents little difficulty to Portuguese learners.

Phonology

Portuguese is a syllable-timed language, in contrast to English. This can result in learners having serious difficulty reproducing the appropriate intonation patterns of spoken English. This is less of a problem for European Portuguese speakers, whose Portuguese variety is stress-timed like English. Portuguese contains about 9 vowel sounds and 19 consonant sounds. This is fewer than English, and there are fewer consonant clusters.

Grammar

Much of the English verb system will be familiar to Portuguese learners since the same features exist in their own language. However, some significant differences exist, which may lead to mistakes of negative transfer. Portuguese word order is a little more flexible than that of English; and there are variations between the two languages in the placement of adjectives, adverbials or pronouns and in the syntax of sentences containing indirect speech. However, basic Portuguese sentence structure is similar to that of English so learners have no especial difficulty expressing their ideas comprehensibly.

Vocabulary

Because of shared Latin roots there are many English/Portuguese cognates, which can facilitate the acquisition of a strong academic vocabulary.

Pronunciation

Pronunciation is arguably the most important aspect of learning a language. Of course, you don't have to be able to pronounce everything perfectly to be understood, and it will take time to get used to the strange sounds that you have to produce.

A few of the sounds in Portuguese can be difficult to imitate at first, because the sounds aren't used in English. But most people can understand what you're saying, even if you don't say every word perfectly. Many people think a foreign accent is charming, so don't worry about it.

There are a few things we must consider to get the Portuguese pronunciation right! Let's start with the easy rules first.

1. Usually in Portuguese, words are stressed in the second to last syllable.
2. Words ending with L, Z, R, U and I, are stressed in the LAST syllable.
3. Written accents are stronger than any other rule.
4. You normally read every single letter in a word, except the H that is always silent.

Portuguese alphabet

Let's start with something really basic, the alphabet

Aa	Bb	Cc	Dd	Ee	Ff	Gg	Hh	Ii	Jj	Kk	Ll
Á	bê	Cê	Dê	é	efe	gê	agá	I	jota	capa	ele

Mm	Nn	Oo	Pp	Qq	Rr	Ss	Tt	Uu	Vv	Ww
Eme	ene	ó	pê	quê	erre	esse	tê	u	vê	duplo-vê

Xx	Yy	Zz
Xis	ípsilon	zê

Portuguese diacritical marks

The tilde [~] – Used to denote a nasal sound

The acute accent [´] – Stress is placed on this syllable, and the vowel sound is open.

The grave accent [`] – Usually denotes 2 words squashed into one with the loss of a letter, but does not really affect pronunciation.

The circumflex accent [^] – Stress is placed on this syllable and the vowel sound is close.

Some letters in Portuguese have different sounds.

Let's start with the vowels:
A – like "a" in "ah"

Á - More open like in "cat"

À – Similar sound as "á" but only used alone, not in a word.

E – "Eh"

Ê – "Eh", but very short, almost silent (similar to French)

É – "Ay", as in "say"

I – "ee", like in "Free"

O – "oo"

Ó - like 'o' in 'hot'

Ô - like 'oa' in 'coal'

U - like the last 'u' in 'kung fu'.

And now let's see the consonants:
C followed by "a,o,u" – K, a "c" that begins a word usually sound like a "k"

C followed by "e,i" – S

Ç – S, if the c has a hook-shaped mark under it, it makes an "s" sound

Ch – sh

G followed by "a,o,u" – hard "g" like in "go"

G followed by "e,i" – zh or J

Gu followed by "a" – gwa

Gu followed by "e,i" - hard "g" like in "go"

J - zh, like the s in "measure"

Lh - Like the "ll" in Spanish pronunciation. There is no English equivalent.

Nh - Just like the Spanish Ñ in "niño", or the French "gn" in "Champagne".

Qu followed by "a,ei" – Kw

Qu followed by "e,I" – K

Some examples

Let's see some sentences. Try reading out loud.

These are normal sentences without diacritical marks.

The bold parts are the ones to be stressed:

- **Co**mo tem pa**ssa**do? (How has he been?)
- **Co**mo ele **co**me a co**mi**da. (How he eats food)
- O **li**vro tem **fo**lhas. (The book has leaves)
- As **fo**lhas do livro **lem**bram **ou**tro livro **ve**lho. (The book's leaves remind me of another old book)
- **E**les **com**pram **jor**nais e re**vis**tas. (They buy newspapers and magazines)
- A **mi**nha **pri**ma tem **ma**is livros do que a **mi**nha vi**zi**nha. (My cousin has more books than my neighbour)

Now let's try examples with diacritical marks.

The diacritical marks are bolded:

- Hoje **é** quarta-feira. (Today is Wednesday)
- O gato subiu **à á**rvore e nunca mais desceu. (The cat ran up the tree, and hasn't come down since.)
- **Não são** permitidos elefantes no bar depois das oito horas. (Elephants are not permitted in the bar after eight o'clock.)
- Duas em cada tr**ê**s pessoas **não** entendem propor**çõe**s em matem**á**tica. (Two after three people do not understand proportions in mathematics.)
- O meu filho **é** um gangster frio e impla**cá**vel, e eu preciso de um abra**ç**o. (My son is a cold-hearted gangster, and I need a hug.)

Some Grammar

If your language is English there are some things in Portuguese grammar that might not be easy for you to understand. So I thought I should add some grammar tips to help you understand.

The good news is that grammar is not really that difficult. You just need to be realistic: it takes a few *years* to really get to grips with a language.

One of the things people don't understand are nouns because when we talk in English about objects we use "it" but in Portuguese we refer to things and animals as people, so they have masculine and feminine.

Nouns and Articles

To say "A", "An", or "Some" in Portuguese, you have 4 possibilities depending on gender and number. Gender, refers to words that are either feminine or masculine. Every single object, idea or person is either masculine or feminine - say male or female.

In English we have "The" as a definite article, but in Portuguese there isn't just one, so let's see how it works.

PT	EN	
O (oo)	The	masculine singular
Os (oosh)	The	masculine plural
A (ah)	The	feminine singular
As (ash)	The	feminine plural

A similar thing happens with the indefinite articles:

PT	EN	
Um (oong)	a or an	masculine singular
Uns (oongsh)	some	masculine plural
Uma (oomah)	a or an	feminine singular
Umas (oomash)	some	feminine plural

So let's see some examples to check if you really got this.

- livro - the book.
- As canetas - the pens.
- rato - the mouse.
- A filosofia - the philosophy.
- Os sonhos - The dreams.
- Um livro - a book.
- Uns livros - some books.
- Uma ideia - an idea.
- Umas ideias - some ideas.
- Uma caneta - a pen.
- Umas canetas - some pens.

Greetings

I don't know about you, but every time I go out of my country I meet new people and sometimes even make friends. Meeting new people or friends starts by greeting them, so let's learn it in Portuguese and the customs of Portugal:

Initial greetings are reserved, yet polite and gracious.

The handshake is accompanied by direct eye contact and the appropriate greeting for the time of day.

Once a personal relationship has developed, greetings become more personal: men may greet each other with a hug and a handshake and women kiss each other twice on the cheek starting with the right.

Let's extend our Portuguese vocabulary and learn how to greet on the different parts of the day:

- Bom dia! (- Good morning/Good day!)
- Boa tarde! (-Good Afternoon!)
- Boa noite! (-Good Evening!/Good night!)
- Olá, como vai? (Hi, how are you?)
- Estou bem, obrigado. (I'm ok, thank you)
- Estou ótimo. (I'm fine)
- Mais ou menos. (Not too bad)
- Meu nome é John, e o seu? (My name is John, and yours?)
- Prazer em conhecê-lo (Nice to meet you.) - If the person you are meeting is a man.
- Prazer em conhecê-lo (Nice to meet you.) - If the person you are meeting is a man.
- Prazer em conhecê-la (Nice to meet you.) - If the person you are meeting is a woman.
- Note: You can mix "Olá" with "bom dia, boa tarde, boa noite" to make another fairly informal greeting (e.g. Olá, bom dia)
- Adeus (Goodbye)
- Chau (Cya)
- Até logo. (See you later)
- Até amanhã. (See you tomorrow)
- Até já (See you soon)
- Até à próxima (See you next time)
- Se faz favor/Por favor (Please)
- Obrigado (Thank you)
- Muito obrigado (Thank you very much)

General Conversation

Now we know how to greet the people we talk with, but it would be a weird conversation if we only say hello and goodbye.

Read through the word lists on the following pages, and practise saying them aloud.

Let's see some simple conversational phrases:

- Aonde você vai? (Where are you going?)
- Qual é o seu nome? (What's your name?)
- Você tem apelido? (Do you have a nickname?)
- Pode me chamar de Bob. (You can call me Bob.)
- Qual é o seu sobrenome? (What's your last name?)
- Como se soletra? (How do you spell?)
- Vou te apresentar uns amigos... (Let me introduce you to some friends...)
- Essa é minha namorada. (This is my girlfriend.)
- Você sabe o nome dela? (Do you know her name?)
- Como ele se chama? (What's his name?)
- Você fala Português? (Do you speak Portuguese?)
- Só um pouquinho. (Just a little bit.)
- Estou aprendendo. (I'm learning.)
- Eu entendo mais do que falo. (I understand more than I speak.)
- Estou começando a aprender... (I've just started to learn it...)
- De onde é? (Where are you from?)
- Vem de onde? (Where are you from (informal)?)
- Estou aqui de férias (I'm here on a holiday)
- Estou a gostar muito (I like it here very much)
- Que idade tem? (How old are you?)
- Tenho ... anos (I'm ... years old)

Numbers

Numbers are a good thing to know, and it's not that hard. If you learn the numbers from 0 to 29 the rest is just the same, quite simple.

Why would you want to know the numbers in Portuguese you might wonder? Well imagine you're in Portugal and want to ask what time the bus comes, you know how to ask it in Portuguese but people are going to answer in the same language so you need to know how the numbers sound.

So what do you say? Ready to learn?

From 0 to 29

0 – zero

1 – um/uma

2 – dois/duas

3 – três

4 – quarto

5 – cinco

6 – seis

7 – sete

8 – oito

9 – Nove

10 – dez

11 – onze

12 – doze

13 – treze

14 – catorze

15 – quinze

16 – dezasseis

17 – dezasete

18 – dezoito

19 – dezanove

20 – vinte

21 – vinte e um

22 – vinte e dois

23 – vinte e três

24 – vinte e quatro

25 – vinte e cinco

26 – vinte e seis

27 – vinte e sete

28 – vinte e oito

29 – vinte e nove

10 – dez

20 – vinte

30 – trinta

40 – quarenta

50 – cinquenta

60 – sessenta

70 – setenta

80 – oitenta

90 – noventa

100 – cem

Large numbers

123 - cento e vinte e três

200 - duzentos

300 - trezentos

400 - quatrocentos

500 - quinhentos

600 - seiscentos

700 - setecentos

800 - oitocentos

900 - novecentos

999 - novecentos e noventa e nove

1000 - mil

1st – 1º primeiro

2nd – 2º segundo

3rd – 3º terceiro

4th – 4º quarto

5th – 5º quinto

6th – 6º sexton

7th – 7º sétimo

8th – 8º oitavo

9th – 9º nono

10th – 10º décimo

Directions & Places

Getting lost is never a good thing, but getting lost in a country you don't understand the language is worst, so you need some way to ask for directions.

Let's now learn how to ask for directions in Portuguese.

- Excuse me, could you tell me how to get to …?(Desculpe, poderia me dizer como chegar a …?)
- Excuse me, do you know where the … is? (Desculpe-me, sabe onde o … é?)
- I'm looking for … (Estou à procura de…)
- Are we on the right road for …? (Será que estamos no caminho certo para …?)
- Is this the right way for …? (É este o caminho certo para …?)
- Do you have a map?(Tem um mapa?)
- Can you show me on the map? (Pode mostrar-me no mapa?)
- Is there a restaurant near here? (Há algum restaurante aqui perto?)
- Where is the nearest drugstore, please? (Onde fica a farmácia mais próxima, por favor?)
- Can you tell me how to get to the train station, please? (Pode dizer-me como chegar à estação de comboios, por favor?)
- How long will it take to get there? (Quanto tempo vai demorar para chegar lá?)
- Does this bus go downtown? (Este autocarro vai para o centro?)

It's not enough to ask where something is or how to go to some place, you need to understand the answer, let's see some traffic vocabulary:

- Left – esquerda
- Right – direita
- Go along … – Vá ao longo
- Cross - atravesse
- Straight on – em frente
- Opposite – contrário
- Near – perto
- Next to – próximo de
- Between – entre
- At the end (of) – no final (de)
- On/at the corner – em/na esquina
- Behind – atrás
- In front of – na frente de
- Around the corner – ao virar da esquina
- Traffic lights – semáforo
- Crossroads – cruzamento

And finally names of places that you might want to find:

- Supermarket – supermercado

- Hospital – hospital
- Store – loja
- City hall – camara municipal
- Bank – banco
- Church – igreja
- Square – praça
- Bus stop – paragem de autocarro
- Club – clube
- Drugstore – farmácia
- Gas station - posto de gasoline
- Police station – Policia
- School – escolar
- College – faculdade
- Bakery – padaria
- Snack bar –café
- Library – biblioteca
- Museum – museu

Transportation

When you go to a foreign country you most likely are going to take public transport at some point, so you need to know the vocabulary.

Let's learn the different types of transport and some transport vocabulary.

Travelling Vocabulary

- Where's the ticket office? – Onde fica a bilheteira?
- Where do I get the ... to Southampton? – Onde apanho o ... para Southampton?
- What time's the next ... to Portsmouth? – A que horas é o próximo...para Portsmouth?
- This ... has been cancelled – Este... foi cancelado
- This ... has been delayed – Este... está atrasado
- Have you ever been to ...? – Alguma vez estiveste em...?
- Yes, I went there on holiday – Sim, fui la nas férias
- No, I've never been there – Não, nunca estive lá
- I've never been, but I'd love to go someday – Nunca fui lá, mas gostava de ir um dia.
- How long does the journey take? – Quanto tempo dura a viagem?
- What time do we arrive? – A que horas chegamos?
- Do you get travel sick? – Costumas enjoar?
- Have a good journey! – Tenha uma boa viagem!
- Enjoy your trip! – Aproveite a viagem!
- I'd like to travel to ... - Gostava de viajar para...
- I'd like to book a trip to ... - Gostava de marcar uma viagem para...How much are the flights? – Quanto custam os voos?Do you have any brochures on ...? – Tem brochuras para...?

- Do I need a visa for ...? – Preciso de visa para...?

Means of Transportation

- (aero)plane(s) - aviões
- (bi)cycle(s) – bicicleta(s)
- Boat(s) – Barco(s)
- Bus(es) - autocarro(s)/onibus
- Car(s) - carro(s)
- Helicopter(s) - helicoptero(s)
- lorry(lorries) - camião
- Moped(s) - scoter(s)
- (motor)bike(s) - mota(s)
- Ship(s) - cruzeiro(s)
- Submarine(s) / sub(s) - submarino(s)
- Tanker(s) - petroleiro(s)
- Taxi(s) - taxi(s)
- Train(s) - comboio(s)/trem
- Tram(s) – elétrico(s)

- Tube train(s)/underground train(s) - metro(s)
- Van(s) - caravana(s)
- Yacht(s) – Iate(s)

Let's learn some additional phrases:

Taxi

- Do you know where I can get a taxi? – Sabe onde posso apanhar um taxi?
- Do you have a taxi number? – Você tem o número do taxi?
- I'd like a taxi, please – Gostava de apanhar um taxi, por favor
- Sorry, there are none available at the moment – Desculpe, não há nenhum disponível de momento.
- Where are you? – Onde você está?
- What's the address? – Qual é a morada?
- I'm ... - Estou...
    - at the Metropolitan Hotel – No hotel metropolitano
    - at the train station – na estação de comboio
- How long will it be? – Quanto vai demorar?
    - quarter of an hour – um quarto de hora
    - about ten minutes – cerca de dez minutos
- Where would you like to go? – Onde gostaria de ir?
    - I'd like to go to ... - Gostava de ir para...
    - Could you take me to ...? – Podia levar-me para...?
- Could we stop at a cashpoint? – Podemos parar num multibanco?
- Is the meter switched on? – O taxímetro est
- How much would it cost? – Quanto custaria?
- Por favor, lige o taxímetro - Please switch the meter on
- How long will the journey take? – Quanto vai demorar a viagem?
- Do you mind if I open/close the window? – Importa-se que abra/feche a janela
- Are we almost there? – Estamos quase lá?
- That's fine, keep the change – Deixe estar, fique com o troco
- Would you like a receipt? – Quer recibo?
- Could you pick me up here at ...? – Podia vir buscar-me aqui às...?
- Could you wait for me here? – Pode esperar aqui por mim?

Bus and Train

At the bus or train station
- Where's the ticket office? – Onde fica a bilheteira?
- Where are the ticket machines? – Onde estão as máquinas de bilhetes?
- What time's the next bus/train to ...? – A que horas é o próximo autocarro/comboio para...?
- Can I buy a ticket on the bus/train? – Posso comprar bilhete no autocarro/comboio?

- How much is a ticket to London? – Quanto custa um bilhete para Londres?
- I'd like a ticket to Bristol – Quero um bilhete para Bristol
- When would you like to travel? – Quando gostava de viajar?
- When will you be coming back? – Quando vai voltar?
- I'd like a return to …, coming back on Sunday – Gostava de um bilhete de ida e volta para…, volto no domingo.
- Which platform do I need for …? – Que plataforma preciso para…?
- Is this the right platform for …? – Esta é a plataforma certa para…?
- Where do I change for …? – Onde mudo para…?
- You'll need to change at … - Você tem que mudra em…
- Can I have a timetable, please? – Posso ter um hórario, por favor?
- How often do the buses/trains run to …? – Com que frequencia os autocarros/comboios vão para…?
- The train's running late – Esse comboio está atrasado
- The train's been cancelled – Esse comboio foi cancelado

On the bus or train

- Does this bus/train stop at …? – Este autocarro/comboio para em…?
- Could you tell me when we get to …? – Pode dizer-me quando chegarmos a…?
- Could you please stop at …? – Pode parar em…?
- Is this seat free? – Este lugar está livre?
- Is this seat taken? – Este lugar está ocupado?
- Do you mind if I sit here? – Importa-se que me sente aqui
- Tickets, please – bilhetes, por favour
- Could I see your ticket, please? – Posso ver o seu bilhete, por favor?
- I've lost my ticket – Perdi o meu bilhete
- What time do we arrive in …? – A que horas chegamos a…?
- What's this stop? – Qual é esta paragem?
- What's the next stop? – Qual é a próxima paragem?
- This is my stop – Esta é a minha paragem
- I'm getting off here – Vou sair aqui
- Is there a buffet car on the train? – Há carruagem com café no comboio?
- This train terminates here – Este comboio acaba a viagem aqui
- Please take all your luggage and personal belongings with you – por favor, leve toda a sua bagaguem e objetos pessoais consigo.

The Tube/subway

- Could you tell me where the nearest Tube station is? – Pode dizer-me onde fica a estação de metro mais perto?
- Where's there a map of the Underground? – Onde há um mapa do metro?

- Which line do I need for Camden Town? – Que linha tenho que apanhar para Camden Town?
- How many stops is it to …? – Quantas paragens são para…?
- I'd like a Day Travel card, please – Queria um cartão diário de viagem, por favor
- Which zones? – Quais zonas?
- Platform – Plataforma
- Waiting room – Sala de espera
- Lost property – Pertences perdidos
- Underground - Subsolo
- Bus stop – Paragem de autocarro
- Request stop – Pedir paragem
- On time – A horas
- Delayed – Atrasado
- Cancelled – Cancelado
- Priority seat – Lugares prioritários

Planes

Checking in

- I've come to collect my tickets – Vim buscar os meus bilhetes
- I booked on the internet – Marquei na internet
- Do you have your booking reference? – Tem a referência da marcação?
- Your passport and ticket, please – O seu passaporte e bilhete, por favor
- Here's my booking reference – Aqui está a minha referência de marcação
- Where are you flying to? – Para onde vai voar?
- Did you pack your bags yourself? – Fez as malas sozinho?
- Has anyone had access to your bags in the meantime? – Alguém teve acesso às suas malas entretanto?
- Do you have any liquids or sharp objects in your hand baggage? – Tem algum liquid ou objetos afiados na sua mala de mão?
- How many bags are you checking in? – De quantas malas vai fazer check in?
- Could I see your hand baggage, please? – Posso ver a sua mala de mão, por favor?
- Do I need to check this in or can I take it with me? – Precisa de ver isto ou posso levar comigo?
- You'll need to check that in – Preciso de verificar isso
- There's an excess baggage charge of … - Tem um excesso de bagaguem, custo adicional de…
- Would you like a window or an aisle seat? – Gostava de lugar à janela ou corredor?
- Enjoy your flight! - Aproveite o voo

- Where can I get a trolley? – Onde posso arranjar um carrinho?

Security

- Are you carrying any liquids? – Tem algum liquido consigo?
- Could you take off your …, please? – Podia tirar o seu…, por favor?
- Could you put any metallic objects into the tray, please? – Pode por qualquer objeto metalico no tabuleiro, por favor?

- Please empty your pockets – Esvazie os bolsos, por favor
- Please take your laptop out of its case – Por favor, tire o seu portátil da bolsa

- I'm afraid you can't take that through – Temo que não possa levar isso.

In the departure lounge
- What's the flight number? – Qual é o número do voo?
- Which gate do we need? – Que porta precisamos?
- Last call for passenger Smith travelling to Miami, please proceed immediately to Gate number 32 – Última chamada para o passageiro Smith do voo para Miami, por favor dirija-se imediatamente para a porta número 32
- The flight's been delayed – O voo está atrasado
- The flight's been cancelled – O voo foi cancelado
- We'd like to apologise for the delay – Gostaríamos de pedir desculpa pelo atraso

- Could I see your passport and boarding card, please? – Posso ver o seu passaporte e cartão de embarque, por favor?

On the plane
- What's your seat number? – Qual é o número do seu lugar?
- Could you please put that in the overhead locker? – Pode por isso no compartimento superior, por favor?
- Please pay attention to this short safety demonstration – Por favor, preste atenção à pequena demostração de segurança
- Please turn off all mobile phones and electronic devices – Por favor, desligue todos telemóveis e aparelhos eletrónicos
- The captain has turned off the Fasten Seatbelt sign – O capitão desligou o sinal de apertar o cinto.
- How long does the flight take? – Quanto dura este voo?
- Would you like any food or refreshments? – Gostaria de alguma comida ou refrescos?
- The captain has switched on the Fasten Seatbelt sign – O capitão ligou o sinal de apertar o cinto
- We'll be landing in about fifteen minutes – Vamos aterrar dentro de quinze minutos
- Please fasten your seatbelt and return your seat to the upright position – Por favor, aperte os cintos e volte para o seu lugar.
- Please stay in your seat until the aircraft has come to a complete standstill and the Fasten Seatbelt sign has been switched off – Por favor, fique no seu lugar até o avião complete a aterrajem e mantenha o cinto até o sinal ser desligado

- The local time is … - A hora local é…

Things you might see
- Arrivals - Chegadas
- Departures - Partidas
- International check-in – Check-in internacional
- Domestic flights – Voos domésticos

- Check-in closes 40 minutes before departure – Check-in fecha 40minutos antes da partida
- Transfers – Transferências
- Baggage claim - Bagagens
- Passport control – Controlo de passaportes
- Customs - Alfândega
- Car hire – Aluger de carroDepartures board – Quadro de partidas

- Gate closed – Porta fechadaArrivals board – Quadro de chegadas.

Eating out

If invited to a dinner party in Portugal, take into account the following:

- Arrive no more than 15 minutes after the stipulated time.
- You may arrive between 30 minutes and one hour later than the stipulated time when invited to a party or other large social gathering.
- Dress conservatively. There is little difference between business and social attire.
- Do not discuss business in social situations.
- If you did not bring a gift to the hostess, send flowers the next day.
- Table manners are formal.
- Remain standing until invited to sit down. You may be shown to a particular seat.
- Table manners are Continental -- the fork is held in the left hand and the knife in the right while eating.
- Do not begin eating until the hostess says "bom apetite".
- Do not rest your elbows on the table, although your hands should be visible at all times.
- Most food is eaten with utensils, including fruit and cheese.
- Keep your napkin to the left of your plate while eating. Do not place the napkin in your lap. When you have finished eating, move your napkin to the right of your plate.
- If you have not finished eating, cross your knife and fork on your plate with the fork over the knife.
- Leave some food on your plate when you have finished eating.
- Indicate you have finished eating by laying your knife and fork parallel on your plate, tines facing up, with the handles facing to the right.

Vocabulary

Eating and drinking

Here are a few expressions you may find useful when arranging to go for a drink or meal, and a couple of signs you may see whilst out.

- Do you know any good restaurants? –Conhece algum restaurante bom?
- Where's the nearest restaurant? – Onde fica o restaurante mais perto?
- Can you recommend a good pub near here? – Pode recomendar um bar aqui perto?
- Do you fancy a pint? – Gostavas de ir beber uma cerveja?
- Do you fancy a quick drink? – Gostavas de ir beber um copo?
- Shall we go for a drink? – Vamos beber um copo?
- Do you know any good places to …? – Conheces algum sitio bom para…?
- Eat – Comer
  - get a sandwich – ir buscar uma sandes
  - go for a drink – beber um copo

- Shall we get a take-away? – Vamos buscar take-away?
- Let's eat out tonight – Vamos comer for a hoje
- Would you like to …? – Gostavas de…?
  - come for a drink after work – vir beber depois do trabalho
  - come for a coffee – vir tomar café

  - join me for lunch – juntar-te a mim para almoço

At pub/bar

Ordering drinks

- What would you like to drink? – Que queres para beber?
- What are you having? – O que estas a beber?
- What can I get you? – O que posso trazer?
- I'll have …, please – Eu quero…, por favor.
  - A beer – uma cerveja
  - a glass of white/red wine – um copo de vinho branco/tinto
  - an orange juice – um sumo de laranja
  - a coffee – um café
  - a Coke – uma cola
- Lots of ice, please – muito gelo, por favor
- A little, please – um pouco, por favor
- Are you being served? – Já está servido?
- I'm being served, thanks – Estou servido, obrigado
- Who's next? – Quem está a seguir?
- Which wine would you like? – Que vinho quer?
- House wine is fine – Vinho da casa serve
- I'll have the same, please Quero o mesmo, por favor
- Nothing for me, thanks – nada para mim, obrigado
- Keep the change! – Fique com o troco
- Are you still serving drinks? – Ainda está a servir bebidas?

Ordering snacks and food

- Do you have any snacks? – Tem aperitivos?
- Do you have any sandwiches? – Tem sandes?
- Do you serve food? – Serve comida?
- What time does the kitchen close? – A que horas fecha a cozinha?
- Are you still serving food? – Ainda serve comida?
- What flavour would you like? – de que sabor quer?
  - really salted – muito salgadas
  - cheese and onion – queijo e cebola
  - salt and vinegar – sal e vinagre
- What sort of sandwiches do you have? – que tipo de sandes tem?
- Do you have any hot food? – Tem comida quente?
- Today's specials are on the board – Os especiais do dia estão no quadro

- What can I get you? – Que lhe posso arranjar?
- Would you like anything to eat? – Quer algo para comer?
- Could we see a menu, please? – Posso ver o menu, por favor?

- Eat in or take-away? – Comer cá ou para levar?

Internet access
- Do you have internet access here? – Tem acesso à internet aqui?
- Do you have wireless internet here? – Tem wireless aqui?
- What's the password for the internet? – Qual é a palavra passe da internet

Smoking
- Do you smoke? – Fuma?
- No, I don't smoke – Não, não fumo
- Do you mind if I smoke? – Importa-se que eu fume?
- Would you like a cigarette? – Quer um cigarro?

At a restaurant

These phrases will help you to make a reservation at a restaurant and order your meal. On arrival it is customary to wait to be seated. On paying it is customary to leave a tip unless a service charge is included or the service has been poor.

Booking a table
- Do you have any free tables? – Tem mesas livres?
- A table for two, please – Uma mesa para dois, por favor
- I'd like to make a reservation – Gostava de fazer uma reserva
- I'd like to book a table, please – Gostava de marcar uma mesa, por favor
- When for? – Para quando?
- For what time? – Para que horas?
- This evening at … - Esta noite às…
- For how many people? – Para quantas pessoas?
- I've got a reservation – Tenho reserve
- Do you have a reservation? – Tem reserva?

Ordering the meal
- Could I see the menu, please? – Posso ver o menu, por favor?
- Could I see the wine list, please? – Posso ver a lista de vinhos, por favor?
- Can I get you any drinks? – Que vai desejar para beber?
- Are you ready to order? – Está pronto para pedir?
- Do you have any specials? – Tem especiais?
- What's the soup of the day? – Qual é a sopa do dia?
- What's this dish? – O que é este prato?
- What do you recommend? – O que recomenda?
- I'm a vegetarian – Sou vegetarian

- I don't eat … - Eu não como…
  - Meat – Carne
  - Pork - Porco
- I'll have the … - Quero …
  - Chicken breast – Peitos de frango
  - Roast beef – carne assada
  - Pasta - massa
- I'm sorry, we're out of that- Desculpe, já não temos isso?
- For my starter I'll have the soup, and for my main course the steak – Para começar quero sopa, e para prato principal quero o bife
- How would you like your steak? – Como quer o seu bife?
  - Rare – mal passado
  - Medium – médio
  - well done – bem passado
- Is that all? – É tudo?
- Would you like anything else? – Vai desejar mais alguma coisa?
- Nothing else, thank you – Mais nada, obrigado
- We're in a hurry – Estamos com pressa
- How long will it take? – Quanto vai demorar?

- It'll take about twenty minutes – Demora cerca de vinte minutos

During the meal

If you'd like to get the waiter's attention, the most polite way is simply to say:

- Excuse me! – Desculpe!

Here are some other phrases you may hear or wish to use during your meal:

- Enjoy your meal! – Aproveite a comida!
- Bon appétit! – Bom apetite!
- Would you like to taste the wine? – Gostava de provar o vinho?
- Could we have …? – Pode trazer…?
  - another bottle of wine – outra garrafa de vinho
  - some more bread – mais pão
  - some more milk – mais leite
  - a jug of tap water – uma jarra de água
  - some water – alguma água
- Would you like any coffee or dessert? – Vai desejar café ou sobremesa?
- Do you have any desserts? – Tem sobremesas?
- Could I see the dessert menu? – Posso ver o menu das sobremesas?
- Was everything alright? – Estava tudo bom?
- Thanks, that was delicious – Obrigada, estava delicioso

- This isn't what I ordered – Isto não é o que pedi
- This food's cold – Esta comida está fria
- This is too salty – Isto está muito salgado
- This doesn't taste right – Isto não sabe bem
- We've been waiting a long time – Estamos a muito tempo à espera
- Is our meal on its way? – A nossa refeição está a caminho?

- Will our food be long? – A nossa comida vai demorar?

Paying the bill

- The bill, please – A conta, por favor
- Could we have the bill, please? – Pode trazer a conta, por favor?
- Can I pay by card? – Posso pagar com cartão?
- Do you take credit cards? – Aceita cartão de crédito?
- Can we pay separately? – Podemos pagar em separado?

Hotel and Accommodation

These expressions may come in useful when choosing an accommodation.

- Can you recommend any good …? – Pode recomendar algum bom…?
  - Hotels - hotel
  - B&Bs –acomodação bed & breakfast
  - youth hostels - hostels
  - campsites – parques de campismo
- How many stars does it have? – Quantas estrelas tem?
- I'd like to stay in the city centre – Gostava de ficar no centro da cidade
- How much do you want to pay? – Quanto quer pagar?
- How far is it from the …? – Qual é a distância do…?
  - city centre – centro da cidade
  - airport - aeroporto
  - station – estação

Making a reservation

These are some of the phrases you will need when making a hotel reservation.

Checking availability

- Do you have any vacancies? – Tem vagas?
- From what date? – Para que data?
- For how many nights? – Para quantas noites?
- How long will you be staying for? – Quanto tempo vai ficar?
  - one night – uma noite
  - a week – uma semana
  - a fortnight – duas semanas
- What sort of room would you like? – Que tipo de quarto quer?
- I'd like a … - Quero um…
  - single room – quarto simples

  - double room – quarto duplo

- I'd like a room with … - Gostava de um quarto com
  - an en-suite bathroom – Casa de banho suite
  - a bath – banheira
  - a shower – chuveiro
  - a view – vista
  - a balcony - varanda

- Could we have an extra bed? – Podemos ter uma cama extra?

Asking about facilities

- Does the room have …? – O quarto tem…?

- o internet access – acesso a internet
- o air conditioning – ar condicionado
- o television - televisão
- Is there a …? – Há…?
  - o swimming pool - piscina
  - o sauna - sauda
  - o gym - ginásio
  - o beauty salon – salão de beleza
  - o lift - elevador
- Do you allow pets? – Permitem animais?
- Do you have wheelchair access? – Tem acesso a cadeiras de rodas?
- Do you have a car park? – Tem parquet de estacionamento?
- The room has a shared bathroom – O quarto tem casa de banho partilhada

Discussing terms

- What's the price per night? – Qual é o preço por noite?
- Is breakfast included? – O pequeno almoço é incluido?
- That's a bit more than I wanted to pay – Isso é mais do que queria pagar
- Can you offer me any discount? – Pode oferecer-me um desconto?
- Have you got anything …? – Tem algo mais…?
  - o Cheaper - barato
  - o Bigger – maior
  - o Quieter - tranquilo
- Could I see the room? – Posso ver o quarto?

Making the Booking

- OK, I'll take it – Ok, aceito
- I'd like to make a reservation – Gostava de fazer uma reserva
- What's your name, please? – Qual é o seu nome, por favor?
- Can I take your …? – Pode dar-me o seu…?
  - o credit card number – número de cartão de crédito
  - o telephone number – número de telefone

Checking in

On arrival at your hotel these expressions will help you when checking in.

- I've got a reservation – Tenho reserva
- Your name, please? – O seu nome, por favor?
- Could I see your passport? – Posso ver o seu passaporte
- Could you please fill in this registration form? – Pode preencher o formulário, por favor?

- My booking was for a double room – a minha marcação foi para um quarto duplo
- Would you like a newspaper? – Quer um jornal?
- What time's breakfast? – Qual é a hora do pequeno almoço?
- Breakfast's from 7am till 10am – Pequeno almoço é das 7 da manhã até às 10 horas
- Could I have breakfast in my room, please? – Posso ter pequeno almoço no quarto, por favor?
- What time's the restaurant open for dinner? – A que horas o restaurante abre para o jantar?
- Dinner's served between 6pm and 9.30pm – O jantar é servido entre as 6 da tarde e as 9 e meia da noite
- What time does the bar close? – A que horas fecha o bar?
- Would you like any help with your luggage? – Quer ajuda com a bagagem?
- Here's your room key – Aqui tem a chave do quarto
- Your room number's … - O seu quarto é o número...
- Your room's on the first floor – O seu quarto é no primeiro andar
- Where are the lifts? - Onde são os elevadores?
- Enjoy your stay! – Aproveite a sua estadia!

Things you might see

- Do not disturb – Não incomudar
- Please make up room – Por favor, arranje espaço
- Lift out of order – Elevador fora de serviço

Checking out

These English phrases will be useful when checking out of a hotel.

- I'd like to check out – Gostava de fazer o check out
- I'd like to pay my bill, please – Gostava de pagar a conta, por favor
- I think there's a mistake in this bill – Acho que há um erro com a conta
- How would you like to pay? – Como gostava de pagar?
- Have you used the minibar? – Usou o minibar?
- Could we have some help bringing our luggage down? – Pode ajudar a trazer a bagagem para baixo?
- Do you have anywhere we could leave our luggage? – Tem algum sitio onde possa deixar a bagagem?
- Could I have a receipt, please? – Pode dar-me o recibo, por favor?
- Could you please call me a taxi? – Pode chamar um taxi, por favor?
- I hope you had an enjoyable stay – Espero que tenha gostado da sua estadia

- I've really enjoyed my stay – Gostei muito da minha estadia

Shopping

Whether you love shopping, or just shop when you need to, you can practice your Portuguese at the same time!

Shopping is a great way to communicate with lots of different people, and it really helps to boost your confidence in speaking Portuguese!

If you familiarise yourself with the phrases and vocabulary in this book, then you'll know what you should expect to hear from the people you talk to on your shopping spree. It'll make shopping a more enjoyable experience, and improve your Portuguese too!

Opening times

- What times are you open? – A que horas abre?
- We're open from 9am to 5pm, Monday to Friday – Estamos abertos das 9 da manhã até às 5 da tarde, de segunda a sexta.
- We're open from 10am to 8pm, seven days a week – Estamos abertos das 10 da manhã às 8 da noite, sete dias por semana
- Are you open on ...? – Estão abertos em/na...?
- What time do you close? – A que horas fecha?
- What time do you close today? – A que horas fecha hoje?
- What time do you open tomorrow? – A que horas abre amanhã?

Selecting goods

- Can I help you? – Posso ajudar?
- I'm just browsing, thanks – Estou só a ver, obrigado.
- How much is this? – Quanto é isto?
- How much are these? – Quanto custam estes?
- How much does this cost? – Quanto custa isto?
- How much is that ... in the window? – Quanto é aquele... na janela?
- That's cheap – Isso é barato.
- That's good value – Isso é um bom valor.
- That's expensive – Isso é caro.
- Do you sell ...? – Você vende...?
- Sorry, we don't sell them – Desculpe, não vendemos isso.
- Sorry, we don't have any left – Desculpe, já não temos.
- I'm looking for ... - Estou a procura de...
- Could you tell me where the ... is? – Podia dizer-me onde ... está?
- Where can I find the ...? – Onde posso encontrar...?
- Have you got anything cheaper? – Tem algo mais barato?
- It's not what I'm looking for – Não é o que procure.
- Do you have this item in stock? – Você tem isto em stock?
- Does it come with a guarantee? – Vem com garantia?

- Do you deliver? – Fazem entregas?
- I'll take this - Vou levar isto
- Would you like anything else? – Gostava de levar mais alguma coisa?

Making payment

- Are you in the queue? – Está na fila?
- Next, please! – Próximo, por favor.
- Do you take credit cards? – Aceita cartão de crédito?
- I'll pay in cash – Pago com dinheiro
- I'll pay by card – Pago com cartão
- Could I have a receipt, please? – Pode dar-me o recibo, por favor?
- Would you be able to gift wrap it for me? – Pode embrulhar?
- Would you like a bag? – Quer um saco?

Returns and complaints

- I'd like to return this – Gostava de devolver isto
- I'd like to change this for a different size – Gostava de trocar por outro tamanho
- It doesn't work – Não funciona
- It doesn't fit – Não serve
- Could I have a refund? – Posso ter um reembolso?
- Have you got the receipt? – Tem o recibo?
- Could I speak to the manager? – Posso falar com o gerente?

Things you might see

- Open - Aberto
- Closed - Fechado
- Open 24 hours a day – Aberto 24 horas por dia
- Special offer – Oferta especial
- Sale - Desconto
- Buy 1 get 1 free – Compre 1 leve 1 gratis
- Half price – Metade do preço
- Out to lunch – Fora para almoçar
- Back in 15 minutes – Volto daqui a 15 minutos

- Shoplifters will be prosecuted - Ladrões de lojas serão punidos

Using a credit card

- Enter your PIN – Introduza o PIN
- Please wait – Por favor, aguarde
- Remove card – Remova o cartão
- Signature – Assinatura

CPSIA information can be obtained
at www.ICGtesting.com
Printed in the USA
LVHW061415030622
720218LV00012B/146